Building Disciples Requires Building Curriculum

Collecting and Classifying Truth for Fulfilling the Great Commission

By

Allen L. Elder

This book is a work of non-fiction. Names and places have been changed to protect the privacy of all individuals. The events and situations are true.

ISBN: 1-4033-9011-8 (e-book)
ISBN: 1-4033-9012-6 (Paperback)
ISBN: 1-4033-9013 4 (Dustjacket)

Library of Congress Control Number: 2002095460

This book is printed on acid free paper.

Printed in the United States of America
Bloomington, IN

1stBooks - rev. 11/26/02

This work and all of it's resulting fruit is dedicated

to the glory of God the Father.

TABLE OF CONTENTS

PREFACE

God has two goals in mind when truth is presented to us. He wants us to receive it into our hearts so it can accomplish it's intended change in our lives. Then, he expects us to reproduce it so others can experience the same change of life. Each Christian has ample opportunity to receive and reproduce the truth. This book is written to encourage and equip those who want to fulfill Christ's great commission by giving them a pattern to follow as they collect, classify, and communicate God's truth.

My prayer for you as you read is that God will use this effort to enlighten you to his purpose and use this method of reproducing truth to multiply your life in fulfillment of his command to make disciples.

Allen L. Elder

Woodruff, South Carolina

ACKNOWLEDGEMENTS

This expression of gratitude is to many people who were instrumental in bringing this work to completion. Thanks to my family, Connie, Trey, Blake, and Scott for their longsuffering with me. To every congregation which have encouraged me along the way. To some of our special partners in the ministry, Randy and Robin Allen, Miriam Cribb, and "Boots" McManus. Special thanks to my dad and the Renfrow Brothers ministry team. And to Ralph Wilborn, whose conversations with me have helped me more than he realizes. Finally, to Herb Hodges who rescued me from the life of a useless Christian by turning me into a reproducing disciple of the Lord Jesus Christ. God bless each one of you.

Allen Elder

PART ONE

BUILDING DISCIPLES

CHAPTER ONE

THE MANDATE

Forty days away from civilization. Forty days among beasts and wild animals. Forty days without food. Then came Satan to Jesus with his alluring propositions. The proposition of provision: "Why don't you turn these stones to bread and have a meal. I know you are hungry." The proposition of protection: "Go ahead and leap from the temple, Jesus. God will take care of you." And, the proposition of prestige: "Worship me and I will give you the world!" What a proposition! The world. Who doesn't want it? Fame, fortune, success. It all sounds so inviting. Yes, Jesus wanted the world but not on Satan's terms. No short-cuts. No substitutes. Only in the terms of his Father. He was not interested in the shallow, self-gratification of the moment. The world he wanted required self-denial, steadfastness, and strategy. That's how he wanted it, and he was willing to wait.

Some three and a half years later, the waiting paid off. Just before his betrayal, arrest and crucifixion, Jesus boldly said, "I have conquered the world." (John 16:33). He was not illusioned, nor was he guessing. By reproducing his life into others just as his Father had done with him, he reaped the benefits of working a carefully designed plan. This was a plan to conquer the world by building world-visionary, world-impacting, reproducing disciples who would be able to reproduce more of the same with a goal to impact the world to the last person on earth, until the end of time. This was the goal to which he constantly calibrated his entire life and ministry (John 17:19). It would also become the marching orders for all those who would follow in his footprints.

OUR PURPOSE: WORLD IMPACT

Between his resurrection and ascension, Jesus gave the assignment of world conquest to his followers. We call it the great commission. He said,

"All power is given unto me in heaven and in earth.

Go ye therefore, and teach all nations,

baptizing them in the name of the Father, and of the Son, and of the

Holy Ghost:

Teaching them to observe all things whatsoever I have commanded

you :

and, lo, I am with you alway,

even unto the end of the world.

Amen.

(Matthew 28:18-20).

He offered them the world on God's terms. They accepted those terms and made a lasting spiritual impact upon it. This commission has been issued to and is binding upon every generation of Christians in the history of the world. The genius of his strategy was simply this: "While you are going about your daily business, make disciples." Not just converts, but fully devoted, reproducing followers of Christ. Jesus did not encumber them with extra duties to add to their busy schedules. He said, "You have to be out in the world anyway in the course of your daily lives. Let this objective of making disciples for world impact be the main objective of all that you do. Recruit and make disciples wherever you are at any given time. Make disciples while you work. Make disciples while you play. Let this be the focus of all that you do, and *I* will give you the world! And, by the way, while you are doing it, I will be with you every step of the way."

THE POWER FOR WORLD IMPACT

Jesus had the authority to make such a radical statement. A close look at the commission shows us that it concerns three issues: power to attempt it, a process by which to accomplish it, and a promise as we attain it. Jesus said, "All power (authority) is given to me in heaven and in earth." (v18). As the representative of the Father, Jesus had been given the authority to issue the command to make disciples for world impact. We obey policemen because of the authority they represent. They are representative of the law of the land with authority to enforce that law. The authority of Christ extends over every place man will ever have any concern: heaven and earth; the here and the hereafter. Christ has the authority to issue the command and gives the authority to those who obey it. So then, whatever we do in fulfillment of that command is sanctioned by the authority of the one who gave it. As we build disciples for world conquest,

God himself sanctions, endorses, and finances all of our efforts. He grants us the authority in which to act.

THE PROCESS OF WORLD IMPACT

Just as Jesus was given this power, or authority, by the Father, he wants to send his reproducing followers throughout the world, sanctioned by this same authority. This authority, however, is only available to those who are following and fulfilling the process of building more reproducing, world-impacting disciples in the same way that Jesus built them. His command is, "Make disciples as you are going by enlisting them into the process of learning to obey my teachings." At this point, the church of today has sadly faltered. Most Christians if they are doing anything at all are only focusing on evangelistic efforts. The command in the commission is not make converts, but make disciples. Evangelism is not an end in itself but is only a part of a much larger scheme. It is actually the first step in disciple-making. Those followers who are evangelizing with a goal to turn the evangelized into world-impacting disciples will fulfill that process with the full authority of the Lord Jesus Christ.

THE PROMISE TO WORLD IMPACTORS

As we go as followers in the power of Christ, fulfilling his plan of building disciples, we receive a special promise. Jesus said, "As you do this, I will be with you." We are not alone as we move out into a dark, lost world. We are on a co-mission: a mission with Jesus Christ.

As long as we follow Christ's instructions, we will enjoy his presence with us to the ends of the earth until the end of time.

Many promises in the Bible are often linked to a process of some kind. This promise is linked to the process of building disciples. The context is not about Christ's presence with us in salvation. We know that once God comes into our spirit, he never leaves or forsakes us. We are saved eternally. Rather, this promise has to do with his purpose for us in service to him. According to this passage, if we are not reproducing disciples for world-impact, we need not expect Christ to be around us very long. He will be with those who are obedient to his Word. His eyes run to and fro throughout the whole earth to show himself strong on behalf of those whose heart is perfect toward him (2 Chronicles 16:9). That explains why the awareness of the presence of Christ is missing in many churches and in the lives of many Christians. How many churches have you visited which were void of the awareness of God's presence? How many Christians have you been around who show little evidence that God lives within them? If they are saved, God is there but if they are not about the Father's business in the world, Christ will not manifest himself through them. In the context of Matthew 28, only those followers who are fulfilling

8

the process of disciple-making can legitimately claim the promise of the presence of Christ with them as they go.

Now, let me ask you. How would you like to know and believe that you can have a strategic impact on the world for Christ? Two persons are offering you the world everyday. And, believe it or not, you are accepting one of those offerings. Be careful, though. You may not always recognize Satan's offer. He is the master of disguise. He knows we cannot turn stones to bread and most of us are not foolish enough to dare God by jumping off of something. But we do fall for provision number three. We accept Satan's offer of the world and end up worshipping him. We may not kill an animal and offer it's body to him in a Satanic ritual. We just mind our own business while the rest of the world perishes, apart from God. We reach for our fleshly desires, our piece of the pie in the sky. We are content with a comfortable house, a nice family, our pets, jobs, or careers and all the things we do to entertain ourselves. I can think of no greater example of someone who has accepted Satan's offer of the world than the comfortable, prospering Christian who goes to church every Sunday but never reproduces one disciple in obedience to the command of Jesus Christ to do so.

On the other hand, God offers the world to us also. He said, "Ask of me, and I shall give thee the heathen for thine inheritance, and the uttermost parts of the earth for thy possession." (Psalm 2:8). The world he offers is a share in what he is doing among the family of mankind. His offer is extended, but few Christians accept it. I hope to call your attention to the voice of God as he extends his offer to you and lead you toward how you can receive it and become all that he intends for you to become.

THE POSSIBILITY OF WORLD IMPACT

The great commission passage is Christ's offer of the world to his followers. Just as he lay the prospect of world conquest before his immediate followers, he offers the same possibility to us today. If we are to achieve it, we will have to be able to see the possibility of world impact from God's point of view.

PAUL'S PRAYER

Praying for the Christians at Ephesus as well as for all generations of believers, Paul said that he was asking the Holy Spirit who lives in our spirits to turn the light on in our hearts to allow us to see three truths from God's point of view. These three truths provide a logical starting place for any Christian who wants to accept Christ's offer of world conquest. Paul prayed that we might know: one, our purpose, or the hope of his calling; two, our potential, or what are the riches of the glory of his inheritance in the saints; and three, God's power working in us to do his will (Ephesians 1:17-19).

OUR PURPOSE

The number of Christians who are unaware of their purpose in the world is staggering. In Jesus' strategy of building disciples, he does not allow for such a discrepancy. He made clear to his followers what is his intention for our lives. "As thou hast sent me into the world, even so have I also sent them into the world." (John 17:18). This is our purpose, or the hope of his calling. Paul told the Thessalonians, "God not only loves you, but has selected you for a special purpose." (1 Thessalonians 1:4)Phillips. Jesus defined that purpose in the selection of his disciples in Mark 3:14. He selected them, and us, I might add, for two reasons: to have a personal relationship with him; and that we might also have a personal ministry for him. God's purpose is that we cultivate an up-close, personal relationship with him so that he might equip us in order to send us throughout the world to do the work he has for us to do. Pay attention to the order. The sending is only to come after the preparation. Herein lies another falter by the church of today. As soon as people are saved, we quickly shove them into positions of service that they are not prepared for. After the inspiration of being saved wears off, and it does according to Hebrews 10:32, they become aware that they are not ready for service and they fall out of the ranks. Jesus' plan is to develop, then deposit the disciple who knows his purpose in the world.

The personal relationship with Jesus is the most significant need in our lives. We never get beyond it, even as we begin to mature as a disciple of Christ. If we are to be used of God in public, we have to have a vital relationship with him in private. Our usefulness in public is limited to the progress we make in our private life with God. A small private life with God results in a small public life for God. Thus, the purpose for our lives is basically two-fold. We are to spend time at God's feet in discipleship then we will be able to spend time on our feet in devoted service to him in fulfilling his mandate to make disciples of every ethnic group on earth.

The hope of God's calling of us is to fulfill the commission by building reproducing disciples. This is the general aim of our public ministries for him. The specific aim of our ministries is that unique way that each one of us has to find in order to accomplish the general aim. Those unique ways are as many as there are people who are doing them. Anything can be turned into a public ministry for fulfilling the great commission.

OUR POTENTIAL

As we are faithful to spend time alone with God, we will soon begin to see how important we are to him and how much potential we have to make a lasting spiritual impact on the world. Usually, when we see the word *inheritance* in the Bible, we are quick to assume that it refers to what we have waiting for us in heaven. However, in this passage, Paul is not speaking of our inheritance in Christ, but of Christ's inheritance in us. Paul said, "I want you to realize that God has been made rich because we who are Christ's have been given to him" (Ephesians 1:18) TLB. Can you believe it? We are part of the reason that God is so wealthy. We can begin to see what great potential we have for God when we realize how important we are to

13

him. The value of something truly lies in the price that we are willing to pay for it. In God's sight, we are worth his Son, Jesus Christ! That is the price that God paid for us. To him, we are worth Jesus. Now, we have a limitless value to the kingdom of God. There is no end to our potential if we will begin to develop it at the feet of a disciple-maker and in our own private time with God. One person has the potential to make a great impact on the world. Just think of the Christians you know of who have done it: Hudson Taylor, Charles Spurgeon, Billy Graham, Dawson Trotman and many more. You have that same kind of potential.

OUR POWER

When a disciple knows his purpose and his potential, he is then ready to experience God's power in his life and ministry. Paul used four different words for power in Ephesians 1:19. If we include the word that Jesus used for power in Matthew 28:18, we get a complete picture of how God does the work of fulfilling the commission through us. God never gives a command without also giving the ability to perform it. When God tells a Moses to cross the Red Sea, he opens it up and dries the ground for the crossing. When God tells a man to stretch forth a withered hand, he restores the hand so the man can stretch it forth. When God tells Peter to get out of the boat, he gives him the ability to walk on water. When God tells a dead Lazarus to step from the grave, he gives life to his body and Lazarus walks out. This is always God's pattern for empowering his people. Paul gave us a glimpse of how it works as seen in the different words he used for power: power, *exousia*, means authority; power, *ischus*, means abiding power; mighty, *kratos*, means applied power; power, *dunamis*, means ability; and working, *energeia*, means action. Put all this together and we see that God's authority abides in us. When it is applied to any task, circumstance or situation, we are given the ability to act as God would act to get through the situation. No wonder Paul could say, "I can do all things through Christ who strengtheneth me" (Philippians 4:13). This power sits ready to be appropriated by any Christian who will obey the command to make disciples.

Everything that we need to impact the world has already been provided for us. Paul again stated this clearly in 2 Timothy 1:9-10. He said that God has given us a purpose to live for, the power to achieve that purpose and a procedure to use to carry out that purpose. With all of this on the table, no Christian has an excuse for not building disciples. Anyone can do it. Every Christian has the potential to impact the world by coping the process that Jesus used to make disciples. Perhaps it will help us get started by looking at some examples from the Scriptures to see the process in action and how we can use it in our own ministries.

CHAPTER TWO

THE MODELS

My favorite genre of film-making is war, especially World War II. As a child, my favorite television programs were *Rat Patrol* and *Twelve O'clock High.* I also loved the old black and white war movies. Now, I like to see these movies to pick out the leadership traits of the heroes. In a scene from *"Enemy At The Gates"*, set in Stalingrad in World War II, Khrushchev is asking his political officers what they think he should do to motivate the men to fight to hold the city from the German invaders. He was given ideas like, "Shoot the generals and their executive officers who fail at their assignment. Deport their families. Make examples out of them." Finally, one man spoke up saying that he should "Give them hope. Encourage them to fight for the love of the Motherland. Make examples for them, yes, but examples to follow. What they need are heroes." What we need today in the church are examples to follow. What we need are heroes. The Bible is replete with examples of men who had others following them, learning from them, and reproducing what they saw. Let's take

a look at some of them.

JESUS

The obvious first hero we need to look at is, of course, Jesus.

Although others built disciples before he did, as Paul said, "It was not

until our Savior, Jesus Christ, was revealed that the method (of

building disciples) became apparent." (2 Timothy 1:9-10) Phillips.

When we look at the life of Christ in the Gospels, we usually only see

the obvious things that standout. We know that he was and is deity.

He was virgin born and raised in obscurity. We know that he was a

great teacher, miracle worker and healer of the sick. We know that he

died on the cross for our sins, was buried and arose from the dead. We

may not understand everything we need to understand about these

obvious subjects but we learn of them by reading the Gospels.

There is one subject, though, that we can read over and over and

probably never see until and unless someone points it out to us. We

hardly consider one of the most important things he did: the training

of his twelve disciples. What he did with them is really much bigger

than training. He reproduced his very life into them. He conveyed who he was and what he had come to do to them and into them until it became real to them. Then, he expected them to reproduce that life into others also.

JESUS WAS SOMEONE'S DISCIPLE

Where did Jesus get such an idea to build disciples? The idea came from his Father. Jesus was merely doing what his Father had done with him. He was himself, a disciple of someone else. Before time began, Jesus was discipled in an up-close, face-to-face relationship with his Father. His followers are not expected to do something that he had not done. By watching his Father, Jesus learned this method of reproducing disciples and copied what he saw him do.

Various passages of Scripture tell us about their relationship in pre-time eternity. Jesus was always at his Father's side like a little child (Proverbs 8:30). He is spoken of as a friend waiting outside his friend's house so they can spend time together (Proverbs 8:34). The constant building and shaping of his life, plan and strategy was learned morning by morning as his ear was awakened to hear as a disciple and as his tongue was taught to speak as a disciple (Isaiah 50:4-5). Until the incarnation, all Jesus had ever known was his face-to-face relationship with his heavenly Father (John 1:1). Of himself, he did nothing, but only those things that he had seen his Father do (John 5:19). In all he did, he had learned to seek his Father's will (John 5:30; 6:38). Everything Jesus did on earth was taught to him by his Father (John 8:28). He was trained as a disciple and sent to represent the Father to the world (John 1:18). His is the prototype of our ministry of making disciples.

JESUS TWO-FOLD WORK ON EARTH

A broad look at the life of Jesus reveals that everything he did can be categorized under two headings. From the cross, he said, "It is finished," literally, "paid in full." (John 19:30). The outstanding debt of sin had been paid and the transaction closed. His sacrifice was once-for-all and forever. Nothing can be added to it or taken from it. His work of redemption in death was finished. This is what the Bible calls the good news. But it is usually the only aspect of Christ's work that we consider. There is another aspect of his work that is worthy of much consideration. Indeed, if he had not done the other work, we would have never heard of his work of redemption.

On the night before his death, Jesus had a long conversation with his Father in prayer (John 17). In this prayer, he did two things. He told us of a second category of his work on earth and he outlined the method he used to carry out that work. Several hours before dying on the cross, Jesus said, "I have finished the work you gave me to do." (John 17:4). He was not yet shedding his life's blood when he spoke these words so he could not have been speaking of his work of redemption. He had to be referring to something else. And, indeed, he was. He was talking about his work of reproducing disciples for world conquest. He had done with each of his close followers, what his Father had done with him. He had reproduced his life in them and was now ready to leave the work in their hands.

JESUS' STRATEGY OF MAKING DISCIPLES

As Jesus continued his prayer, he told us how he was able to make the statement, "I have conquered the world." (John 16:33). It began with the realization of how he was to *increase* the value of God throughout the world of men: "I have glorified thee on earth." (John 17:4a). We are all born for the purpose of bringing glory to God through our lives. In ourselves, we are nothing. But a nothing can either increase or decrease the value of God to others, depending upon how he aligns himself in relation to Jesus Christ. A zero placed in front of the number, one, severely decreases it's value by a multiple of ten. If the zero is placed after the one, it increases it's value ten-fold, a second zero, a hundred-fold. We do the same with the value of Jesus everyday. If we promote ourselves before Christ, we decrease his value in the public life around us. If he comes first in our lives, his value can easily be seen by others. This is how Jesus chose to live in relation to the Father. He wanted the value of the Father to increase as a result of his life.

This increase would be accomplished by the *investment* of his life into the men who would carry on the work after he was gone: "I have finished the work (of building disciples) that you gave me to do." (John 17:4b). So many people today think the ultimate goal of their ministry is to do whatever it is that they do. If theirs is a preaching ministry, they think the ultimate goal is to preach. If theirs is a music ministry, they think the goal is to sing, play the instruments or write songs. However, the goal of every ministry is to make disciples by means of that ministry. Preaching , singing, and everything else are not ends in themselves but the means to an end. Our ministries are to be used to emerge disciples then we are to invest our lives into each one, bringing them up in the Lord until they can reproduce as well. It does not matter how successful our ministries may be from a human standpoint if we are not reproducing disciples. Jesus was not thinking, "I have finished the work of healing the sick," or "I have finished the work of performing astonishing miracles like walking on water or raising the dead." He was thinking, "I have finished the work of building these men into world-impacting, reproducing disciples. Now, they are equipped to carry on the work to the world today and to the next generations." The real tell-of-the-tape in our ministries will never be, "How many sermons did we preach?" But, it will be, "How many disciples did we make by investing our lives into them?"

As Jesus spent time with his men, investing his life into them, he *imitated* what he had seen his Father do with him: "I have manifested thy name unto the men which thou gavest me out of the world." (John 17:6a). This may well uncover one reason so few Christians today are reproducing disciples. Many have never seen a reproducing disciple-maker at work. We have not had someone to give us anything to pass on to others. That is not to say that pastors have not delivered great sermons or that teachers have not taught wonderful lessons. They have. But they have not done it from a strategic, disciple-making point of view. No one in the church today is expected or required to reproduce what they are given. Pastors deliver their sermons, people sit through them, but no reproduction takes place. That is why much religious activity around the church house today is nothing short of "spiritual fornication". We go through the motions, but reproduce no reproducing, world-impacting offspring. Many pastors have fallen into this trap since they have had no one to enlist them into an up-close, personal relationship, thus, they have no one to imitate. Jesus just copied what his Father had done with him. We need a leader that we can copy, too.

Now that Jesus knew what to do and how to do it, he *instructed* them. He pointed them to what God had said on various subjects: "For I have given unto them the words (rhema) which thou gavest me." (John 17:8). Jesus spoke to his disciples concerning various topics that God addressed in his Word. He had declared unto them all the counsel of God, giving them all things that pertained unto life and godliness. His teaching exemplified the fact that the Word of God is profitable for instruction in righteousness. Stated as such or not, every statement he made was substantiated by "It is written". As Jesus built his disciples, he pointed them to the instruction of the Word as a means of equipping them for the work they would have to do. Recently, a young lady asked me about how to have daily devotions with God, or, how to have a quiet time. I suggested that she begin with prayer and reading a passage from the Bible. Her response was, "What a concept! I never thought of reading the Bible!" God instructs us according to his Word. Therefore, it should not come as a surprise that we should have to read it. Reading the Bible, or anything else for that matter, requires discipline. We have to have a regular intake of the Word of God that we might be instructed thereby.

Jesus' relationship with his disciples was also characterized by *intercession*: "I pray for them." (John 17:9). I was once asked to speak at a Women's Missionary Union Conference in the association of churches where I pastored. The theme for the evening was *Praying for the World*. They were surprised when I read this verse as my text where Jesus said, "I pray not for the world. What did Jesus mean by this and why were we there in conference about world prayer if Jesus said that he was not praying for the world. Jesus taught us that the best way to reach the world is by impacting the lives of the individuals around us. By doing this, we can multiply throughout the world and have more influence. If we are going to do this, we have to realize that we cannot mass produce converts and consider the job to be done. This, as far as God's purpose on earth right now is concerned, results in shallow, untrained Christians who are still not able to make a difference in the world. Jesus showed us that the greatest thing we can pray for in regards to the world is for disciples who are capable of leading others to reproduce others still and the greatest thing we can do for the world is to make a reproducing disciple. This is the end toward which Jesus prayed and is what we need to adjust our ministry of intercession toward also. The best way to impact the world is to pray for a person through whom you can reproduce your life in Christ. Who is the individual that you are praying for today through whom you will extend your life to the world?

The process of building disciples requires *intimacy*: "I kept them." (John 17:12b). Jesus knew all of the traps that were set for the disciples and the alluring baits that could easily attract each one away from his purpose for their lives. On one occasion, he told Peter of Satan's desire to sift him as wheat, but he said, "I have prayed for you." As the good shepherd, he guided the flock, keeping his eye on them, losing only the one who was designed to be lost in fulfillment of the Scriptures. Intimate discipling relationships require a certain amount of guard duty as we keep watch over the disciples until their own vision has developed enough to see the dangers that lie so close at hand.

He gave them *insight*: "I have given them thy word (logos)." (John17:14a). Jesus was careful to use two specific words for "word" in verses eight and twelve. The first word speaks of instruction, the second, *logos*, speaks of insight. He not only told the disciples what God had said on various topics, but he also helped them to understand what he meant by what he said. Through living personality, he conveyed a deeper understanding of God as he himself is called, the *Logos*, the Word. The placement of the elements of his process of building disciples reveals how he was able to do this. Between instruction and insight are intercession and intimacy. As he lovingly kept them under his watchful eye and prayerful heart, they were compelled to receive his words. Once, after some superficial followers stopped following him, Jesus asked the disciples if they, too, would also go away. Peter said, "Where can we go? Only you have the words of life." (John 6:68). While they were instructed from

27

the written Word, they were gaining insight from the living Word who had brought the Word of God to life before their eyes. Sharper than a double-edged sword and as skillfully as a master surgeon, his living example pierced the deepest parts of their being, allowing his brilliant insight to illuminate the dark places of their minds. This happened in their private times together. After Jesus had taught , often times, the disciples would later ask some question about his teaching and he would expound all things to them in private. (Mark 4:34). Insight is best gained as we spend time in the presence of the Lord in a private relationship with him.

Jesus left no doubt about his *intention* for his followers: "As thou hast sent me into the world, even so have I also sent them into the world." (John 17:18). Disciples need to know quickly what is the intention of our relationship with God. He intends to send us to the world. Have you noticed how often the Bible mentions people, nations, generations, and the world? It is on almost every page. How is it, then, that in our churches, few people are personally carrying out a ministry that is purposely aimed at the world and at the generations of people who are yet to be born? Who do you know personally who is investing his life like this? We are led to believe that God's intention for those he saves is to wrangle over a few positions on the church organizational chart and those who do not make it this year will just have to hope they will be voted in next year, or the following year, or the year after that. Thank God for those who work in the church to do all the necessary things that have to be done. But somewhere along the line, we have to see that the bulk of ministry is outside the walls of the local assembly. That ministry is in the mills, plants, and factories that we go to on a daily basis. That ministry is in the restaurants, grocery stores, gas stations, and ball fields that we frequent day after day. That ministry is to every ethnic group wherever we find them, across the street or across the ocean. Just as God told Jeremiah, "I have chosen you to be a prophet to the nations of the world." (Jeremiah 1:5). God's intention is that the church gathering place be used as a base of training to equip the saints of God to go out into the world outside and win and build disciples as we go about our daily affairs. Since we know little about God's intention for us, many of us never intend to do anymore than go to church and be proud of how good we are, especially when we see the people of the world and the kind of messes they find themselves in. As I heard a preacher say in a pastor's conference, " We say, we are willing to go, but in reality, we are planning to stay." The truth is that many Christians do not intend to go to the world, even though the one they call Lord has commanded it. I actually had a deacon to say this to me on one occasion. Some of the leadership of this church did not want to reach out to others in their community who were different than they. I pointed out the intention God has to send us to the world. The deacon said, "We do not doubt that that is in the Bible." I said, "You're just not going to do it, is that correct?" He answered, "That's right. We're not going to do it." God's intention is to send us as his representatives to the world. The sooner we accept that divine intention, the more we will see God at work, fulfilling his promise to be with us in our ministries.

I had been saved for twenty years before anyone personally helped me to see this. That is not to say that we were not in church or that we never heard about missionary work. It is to say that it never became personal to me until I met a man to whom the great commission was the intent of his life. Being around a man who had a vision for the world caused me to catch a vision for the world, too. How many others in our churches have wasted years by not knowing the intention God has for our lives? We think, "I just hope that somehow, some way, I can have a little influence on someone." God never meant for the Christian's life to have such miserable odds at making a difference. Rather, he guarantees that we can make a difference on a global scale by learning and following his intention for us.

Jesus' plan includes a guaranteed *impact* on the world if we will follow the plan: "Neither pray I for these alone, but for them also which shall believe on me through their word." (John 17:20). The world offers many ways to measure the impact of a person's life. How much money was he worth? How many games did he win as a starter? What was his invention that has made life more convenient for all of us? What record did she break? How successful was her business? How much land did she own? The list is inexhaustible. But the world never mentions what God considers to be the measure of impact of a person's life; his offspring. How many books have you read about the parents of George Washington, Ben Franklin or Thomas Edison? Jesus emphasizes that the impact of the Christian's life can be seen in his spiritual offspring. It is not primarily seen in how many books we write, sermons we preach, or even souls we win in personal evangelism. Impact is seen in whether or not we reproduced any reproducing disciples. Have you left behind, on purpose, anyone who can reproduce and represent you after you leave this world? What is it that you are banking on as the measure of the impact of your life? Spiritual offspring is required, expected, and guaranteed as we skillfully use the process of disciple-making that Jesus modeled before us.

Finally, Jesus mentioned his own continuing *involvement* with us as we go: "I have declared unto them thy name and will (continue to) declare it." (John 17:26). As we go about our daily business, fulfilling Christ's mandate to make disciples, he has promised to be with us. Each time we work for him, he works through us, continuing to declare the Father's name to the ends of the earth.

It has been said that Jesus did not have a strategy as he lived his life on earth. This is how many Christians live their lives. Consequently, we have little impact to show for it. We set our aim so low and just hope we will hit something significant by accident. Jesus does not accept such a poor effort from us because he gave us a much higher standard and even told us, step by step, what to do. On the contrary, everything he did was according to a strategy that guaranteed world-impacting results. He was careful to outline the strategy of disciple-making in his prayer to the Father before he died on the cross. Using this strategy for world conquest, Jesus reproduced disciples who were able to continue his work in his visible absence from earth. Our lives can have the same kind of impact today as we also follow his plan.

BARNABAS

One of the most noteworthy examples of disciple-making in the Bible is that of a man named Joses. He was such an encouragement to the new church that the apostles nicknamed him Barnabas which means "son of consolation". From man's perspective, we usually think of Barnabas as always working behind the scenes, never a front runner. But from God's perspective, he was always on the front lines, fulfilling the commission without the glare of the spotlight. Without drawing attention to himself, he became a master of Jesus' process of personal disciple-making. He was a patient and meticulous trainer who skillfully discovered, developed and deployed disciples who could and did impact the world. His two greatest reproductions were Saul, who was transformed into Paul, and John Mark.

Several observations can be made that led to the success of Barnabas as a disciple-maker. First, he approached every task from a strategic perspective. He knew that if his life was to have an impact on the world, he would have to work at it. I once saw a statement on a calendar that said, "Some people dream of success while others wake up and work hard at it." No world-impacting disciple-maker ever just wakes up one morning to instant success. Success only comes as a result of investing our lives daily and strategically into Christ's global cause. To Barnabas, his objective was clear. He had to approach everything from the perspective, "What affect will this action have on my fulfillment of the great commission?"

His perspective made it necessary to have long-term goals. Reproducing discipleship is a multiplying effort that begins small but grows exponentially over time. Barnabas did not settle for quick results and refused to take short-cuts. He was in it for the long run, knowing that although he would not live long enough to see the final outcome, it was no less guaranteed.

Perspective also means that one must be willing to take a lesser role for a greater ministry. Barnabas was willing to do that. While he had an extensive public ministry, his greatest work can be seen in the building of two personal disciples, and there is no reason to assume that he did not have others. When everyone else was afraid of Saul, the new convert to Christianity, Barnabas spoke up on his behalf before the apostles. Some ten years after the apostles had put Saul on a slow boat back home to Tarsus, Barnabas went there, digging him out of the woodwork, enlisting him to go with him to Antioch. It was there for one year that Saul learned from Barnabas as they taught other new Christians. Barnabas took Saul on a mission trip to Jerusalem then turned him loose on his own shortly after departing on what we call Paul's first missionary journey.

John Mark had a habit of running when the heat was on. He is the one who ran completely out of his clothes from the mob that came to arrest Jesus in Gethsemane (Mark 14:51-52). Shortly after Paul's first missionary journey began, the same John Mark who was traveling with Paul and Barnabas, left them high and dry in Perga. He may have ran again because the heat was on or because he did not want to submit to Paul's authority as the new team leader. Later, when Paul and Barnabas planned to set out on a second missionary trip, Barnabas wanted to invite John Mark to go with them. Paul refused, the team split, going in two directions. Barnabas went to Cypress and guess who went with him? John Mark. Barnabas was able to disciple him up-close and personally, finally getting him to stay in the fight when the heat was on and to accept authority and accountability. Paul testified to this success when he later confessed, "Mark is profitable to me in the ministry." Although Barnabas has no Biblical writings certainly attributed to him, a look at the New Testament table of contents confirms the kind of impact this man had. Some sixty-five percent of New Testament writings are accredited to his disciples, Paul and Mark, and Luke, his grandson in the faith. This kind of impact only happens as one invests his life into others from a strategic perspective.

A second aspect of the discipling ministry of Barnabas is that he was deeply interested in people. In fact, that is what discipling is all about. It is about people, not programs. Barnabas truly had a heart for people. He always had an eye out for the teachable person. When he met someone, he obviously kept a mental file of them. He kept Saul in mind for years, remembering him when he was sent to evaluate the work to be done in Antioch. Realizing the work was too much for one man, aware of his responsibility to make disciples, seeing the perfect environment for disciple-making in Antioch and finding Saul, he reproduced his life into and through one of the greatest Christians who has ever lived. He recognized the potential of individuals and worked to develop them even when others would have written them off. Saul was written off by the apostles. Mark was written off by Paul. But Barnabas focused on their potential, helping to transform them into world-impacting disciple-makers.

Barnabas was also very persistent in his efforts to help transform his men. He believed so strongly that with the right guidance, Saul could become a great contributor to the work. With a few rough edges knocked off, John Mark really could be profitable to the ministry. Barnabas knew that each individual should have the opportunity to reproduce but that only a persistent leader could take them to that point. Thus, by strategic perspective, being interested in people, and showing steadfast persistence with them, Barnabas walked into the halls of fame as one of the premiere disciple-makers of the New Testament, second only to Jesus Christ himself.

PAUL

Named after the first king of Israel, raised as a devout religionist, trained at the feet of Gamaliel, a Pharisee, a Hebrew of the Hebrews, and a persecutor of Christians, Saul had a personal encounter with Jesus Christ and became a new creation. All of a sudden, who he was, and all he had worked for were instantly made null and void. His life had taken a one hundred-eighty degree turn. He was saved, but what next? Saul had a new life, a new start, and a new direction but still an old way of doing things. All he knew was the in-your-face, my way or the highway, approach to bringing others over to his point of view; a legalistic, mechanical life of do's and don'ts. As a new Christian, he began with the same style he had used in the old life. Except now, instead of his having others killed who would not agree with him, others wanted to kill him. Saul was very convincing in his arguments but left his listeners in a rage. Time after time, they plotted to kill him. Once, after such an episode, the disciples had to go as far as lowering him down the wall of the city in a basket at night so he could escape with his life. Even this was not enough to teach Saul a lesson because he did it again. Finally, the apostles had had enough. They sent him back to where he came from. These were the same men who were personally trained by Jesus. Even the best can overlook a potential disciple if they are not carefully following the multiplication procedure. This oversight on their part cost Saul a number of years of

38

valuable ministry. Finally, one man was willing to take the risk with Saul and that made all the difference in his life. Often times, God uses one individual to steer us in the right direction. Since we are conditioned toward expecting many people to respond to our need and run to our aid, that one person is often missed altogether. Barnabas was the one man making a difference in Saul's life.

When Saul was sent back home to Tarsus, he experienced what many new Christians today go through. When the inspiration of being saved wears off after a short time, we realize that we have a job to do but do not know how to do it or even where to begin. Unless another person steps up, or enlists us, to follow them as they follow Christ, we will fumble around just trying to find something to do for God that we can tolerate instead of that specific thing God has planned for us to do. If we cannot find something to tolerate, we will just give up to trying to be a good Christian and survival becomes our preoccupation Barnabas rescued Saul from that uselessness simply by asking him to work with him in Antioch, watch what he did, learn from him and copy what he saw. For one year, they worked and ministered together among the Christians in Antioch. While that year was important for that church, it was all important for Saul. During that year, as

Barnabas discipled him, he was transformed from Saul into Paul. Because of an up-close, personal relationship with Barnabas, Paul learned what Jesus meant by putting new wine into new wineskins. He went from being useless to the kingdom to being useful to all generations to come.

The accurate measurement of any Christian's impact will never come as the result of our flying by the seat of our spiritual pants. We must be transformed from Saul to Paul in a reproductive, multiplying relationship with a pace-setting Barnabas. Then that measurement will be seen in our training of other reproducing disciples. Paul became a personal trainer of disciples all over the world. He went from people trying to kill him to a person others would be willing to die for. He loved and cared for his disciples as a father for his children. He wrote personal letters of instruction and exhortation to them. In the last chapter of Romans alone, he mentions the names of some thirty people or groups of people that he had a personal interest in. Timothy was one of his most precious disciples. He charged him that he should take what he had given him along with other witnesses, and deposit it into the lives of faithful men who would be able to teach others also (2Timothy 2:2). Paul fully expected Timothy to reproduce disciples as he had taught him, just as he had learned from Barnabas. By the training of other disciples, Paul learned and taught that anyone's life can have an impact on the world to the last person on earth, until the end of time

LUKE

What on earth could possibly be attractive enough to lead a medical doctor to lay aside his practice and invest his life toward another cause? That is exactly what Dr. Luke did. That which was so attractive was a person who was eaten alive with a passion to fulfill the great commission and that passion was contagious. Luke became a disciple and traveling companion of Paul. They shared together as disciple-maker and disciple, each contributing to the other's relationship with God and ministry for God. As Paul was to Barnabas, so Luke was a great disciple of Paul, and world-impacting disciple-maker. He not only accompanied Paul in his travels, but also willingly accepted the assignment to stay in Philippi to build up the Christians in the church that met in the house of Lydia. He also shared in Paul's adventures, being shipwrecked with him at least one time. He went on to achieve greatness in his own right as a maker of disciples.

One of Luke's disciples was a Greek nobleman named Theophilus. Luke went to amazing lengths to collect and present to him an accurate account of the person, plan, and passion of the Lord Jesus Christ. In fact, Dr. Luke called the account an autopsy. He wrote two personal letters to this man, Luke and Acts, one telling him how to have a personal relationship with the Lord Jesus Christ, the other, telling him how to have his own world-impacting ministry for Christ. Approximately twenty-five percent of the volume of New Testament writings were written by one individual to another individual in an effort to evangelize and disciple him. The fact that Luke had learned and mastered the process is clearly seen in these two documents that have been divinely preserved in our New Testament.

CONCLUSION

The Bible is filled with other examples of disciple-makers and disciples like Jesus, Barnabas, Paul, and Luke. They also had their opportunity to conquer the world. These examples were not intended to just be great Bible stories or religious history lessons. They were given to illustrate the outworking of the Lord's commission in the lives of his followers. While many examples could also be given today, there are still not enough Christians who are building reproducing disciples. God has given us the same possibility of world conquest. As Peter said, "We have been given a faith as valuable as theirs." What we need are people who are willing to follow someone else, learn the process, and then use it. What we need are trained people who become leaders who will say, "Follow me, as I follow Christ." We need examples, yes; but, examples to follow. What we need are heroes who will champion the cause of Christ to the ends of the earth until the end of time. The next chapter shows us the best environment where this transformation of disciples can take place; within an up-close, personal relationship.

CHAPTER THREE

THE METHOD

It has been said that everything in life can be traced to a habit. If we are unsuccessful, it can be traced to a habit that has caused it. Likewise, if we are successful, that, too, can be traced to a habit. There are two habits, or practices, that all Christians must have if we are to be successful in fulfilling our Lord's great commission. First, we must make it a habit to cultivate a personal relationship with the Lord Jesus Christ every day of our lives. Then, we must also cultivate a personal relationship with a disciple-maker. These two practices are indispensable for the follower of Christ. How can we become what we ought to become if we do not follow Christ? And, how can we follow Christ if we are unwilling to follow another person? In this chapter, we will take a look at each of these two life-changing disciplines.

THE PERSONAL RELATIONSHIP

The life that Christ would have us live as world-impacting disciples necessarily falls into two categories: our private life with

Jesus, and our public life for Jesus. Several Scriptures bear this out. I like to arrange them in chart form as follows.

PASSAGE	PRIVATE LIFE	PUBLIC LIFE
1. (1Thessalonians 1:4) PT	God not only loves you	but has selected you for a special purpose.
2. (John 19:30; 17:4) KJV	It is finished.	I have finished the work...
3. (Psm 67:2) TLB	Lord, send us around the world with news of thy saving power...	and of thy eternal plan for all mankind.
4. (Mark 3:14) KJV	And he ordained (chose) twelve, that they should be with him...	and that he might send them forth to preach.

I have tried to condition myself to look for this pattern as I read the Scriptures. Amazingly, it is found over and over again throughout the Bible. It teaches us that if God is able to use us to great lengths by sending us into the world, we first have to be prepared for that mission. It has already been stated that too often we fail by sending new Christians to the work when they have never been trained for the work. There is absolutely no substitute for sitting at the feet of Jesus in a personal relationship with him in preparation for the work he wants to send us to do.

One of my favorite Bible characters and writers is David, king of Israel. He stated this principle in one of his recorded prayers. "As for me, I will behold thy face in righteousness: I shall be satisfied, when I awake, with thy likeness." (Psalms 17:15).This verse speaks of the personal, private relationship with Jesus. David began by noting two responsibilities we have in our private time with God. It all begins with a *personal decision* to spend time alone with God. He said, "As for me". We may look at others who have a vital relationship with Christ but that is no good for us. We have to make that decision for ourselves and follow through with it on a regular basis. No short-cut will suffice. When I became serious about wanting to know God and his Word, I wanted to find a book that had all the answers to every question about the Bible. What I really wanted was for someone else to have figured it all out for me. I soon found out that there is no such book. And , there is no substitute for personal Bible study and wrestling for the answers with God in a personal way. Only the Bible itself in conjunction with the Holy Spirit has all the answers and we have to read and study it if we are to find them. It is good to read devotional books and commentaries about what God has said to others in their private time with him. But there is no replacement for what God wants to say personally to us as we spend time alone with him. God wants to speak to each one of us individually. He may want to say something to us that he has not said to another. He may want us to begin a ministry that no one else has ever thought of. We certainly do not want to forfeit that possibility by not making private time for God in our own personal lives. We must decide for ourselves that we will do this.

Next, David said there is a *practical discipline* in our private time with God. "I will behold thy face in righteousness". In our private time with God, we can look into the Word of God and see how Jesus worked in the lives of others. This reveals at least two important truths to us. It shows us more of who Jesus really is and what he is like. His character, person and plan is shown in the way he moves in people's lives and circumstances. Then, it shows us how God is working in our own lives. Bible study is not just academic, to learn verbatim what God has done for others. It is to be dynamic so we can trace his hand in our lives today as well. As we behold his face in righteousness in the Word, through other's lives, it becomes clear to us what God is doing in and around us and what he ultimately wants to do through us. Jesus told Martha that while serving is important, the most important thing we can do is to sit at his feet, get to know him, and see how he wants our lives to align with all he is and what he is doing. Then, we will learn to serve him by doing the specific service he designed for us to do.

These two responsibilities will produce wonderful results as we consistently perform them. The first result that David mentions is *perfect delight*. "I shall be satisfied". Satisfaction seems to be one of the elusive dreams of many Christians. We look for it all the time, but it always seems to be just out of reach. We look for it in a dozen places, but can never apprehend it. Real satisfaction, for the Christian, can only be found in one place. Jesus said, "I am the life" (that you may be satisfied with no one or anything else but me). Only Jesus can satisfy us. He has done everything that is needed for our satisfaction. He redeemed us. He has designed a specific place for us in his body. He has gifted us to fill that place. He has given us a purpose to live for in making disciples and he has given each of us a particular job to do in order to fulfill the great commission. We will only be satisfied as we align ourselves with him and his program, finding out what is that one thing that he wants us to do for him.

Another result that David stated is that of *personal development*. "When I awake". I once heard Mike Murdock say on television , "It only takes a moment to get ready for heaven. But it takes a lifetime to get ready for earth". This is the idea that David conveys in this verse. Conversion is enough to take us to heaven but transformation is what we need in order to be salt and light in the world in which we now live. After we are born again by the Spirit of God, we begin a process that transforms us from what we are to what God wants us to become. Abram had to be transformed to Abraham. Sarai had to be transformed to Sarah. Jacob had to be transformed to Israel. Levi had to be transformed to Matthew. Simon had to be transformed to Peter. Saul had to be transformed to Paul. We have to be developed in our new life in Christ to the place where we stop living out of the old perspective, desires and pursuits and start living according to God's plan for our lives. It is a glorious transformation, and once it is done, we wonder, "How did I ever live any other way?" Personal development is a personal awakening to what the Christian life is really all about.

A final result that Davis spoke of is *perpetual design*: "with thy likeness". Paul also said that God is in the process of conforming us to the image of Christ. (Romans 8:29). "With thy likeness" does not mean that we will all physically look like Jesus. It means that we will all live and act like he lives and acts. His thoughts are to be our thoughts. His plan is to be our plan. His purpose is to be our purpose. The likeness of Christ means that we are in the constant pursuit of all that God wants for our lives. In his likeness, we will have on our heart what God has on his heart. In his likeness, we will live for the purpose of using our lives to build disciples of Christ by all that we do. Thus, the ultimate goal of cultivating a personal relationship with Christ is to live as he lived. That becomes possible as he is able to live not only in us, but through us.

As we are transformed in our personal, private time with the Lord Jesus Christ, we are prepared for the public ministry that he wants to send us to do on his behalf. God has to do a work in us before he will do a work through us. I am convinced that God's will for our lives consists of one thing that he wants us to do. In the finding of that one thing, there are several things we must keep in mind.

God's purpose is the same for every Christian. That purpose is to fulfill the commission of making disciples of every ethnic group to the last person on earth, until the end of time. Any ministry that stops short of this goal is missing God's intended purpose for it. Any ministry that is not working from this perspective should be adjusted to it or scrapped altogether. Making disciples of Christ is the only command within the commission.

We must also keep in mind that each Christian has been given a predominant spiritual gift (Romans 12:6-8). It is all important that we know what our gift is because it defines us to other people. Christians are the way they are largely because of the gift they have. We can know and understand one another better if we look at each other from a spiritually gifted standpoint. Our gift also defines our place in the body of Christ and determines what our personal ministry of fulfilling the commission should be.

Finally, we should know that anything can be used as a ministry for the Lord. Finding the one thing that God wants us to do is not all that difficult. We have to have the right perspective, know our gift, identify our heart's desire, and develop it into a ministry for God. We often waste too much time thinking that ministry has to be so different from everything else that we do. We can do what we love to do as a ministry if we do it with a goal of making disciples for Christ. All of this can be hammered out in our personal, private time with the Lord Jesus Christ.

THE PERSONABLE RELATIONSHIP

A second indispensable that God uses in his method of building disciples in addition to a personal relationship with Jesus is a personable relationship with a disciple-maker. I also heard Mike Murdock say on television, "God uses experience to teach those who are too ignorant to sit at the feet of a mentor." God's method of disciple building involves one-on-one relationships between disciple-makers and disciples. When Philip asked the Ethiopian eunuch who was reading from the prophet Isaiah, if he understood what he was reading, he answered, "How can I, except some man should guide me?" Paul's invitation on several occasions was, "Follow me, as I follow Christ." He said, "Copy me, as I copy Christ himself."

Building disciples requires that we cultivate personable relationships with other people. Paul told us that Christians can be one of two kinds of people in our influence of others: wicked imposters or world impactors (2Timothy 3:1-11). Those who impact the world build personable relationships just like Paul had with Timothy. In verses ten and eleven, Paul listed eleven qualities to be found in a personable relationship. It is in this environment that we reproduce our lives into those who are willing to follow us as we follow Christ. Take a look at these qualities.

The beginning place of spiritual reproduction is *doctrine*. What we believe is all important. There are so many false teachings prevalent today that we need to convey through personable relationships correct Bible doctrine. One of the most important times in my life was a three year period that I spent studying the Bible and being grounded in Biblical doctrine. This is the anchor that holds us, keeping us from being tossed about by every wind of doctrine that blows across the sea of life. Second, manner life has to be related. Manner of life is how we live or behave. Belief comes first, then behavior. What we believe determines how we behave. That which is in the heart eventually comes out in the way we live. To some degree, we can tell what a person believes by the way he behaves. Jesus said a tree can be known by it's fruit. We are known by the fruit we produce with our behavior.

The next thing Paul related to Timothy was his *purpose* or intention for all that he did. Paul knew where he was going and what he was doing. This made him attractive to others, making them willing to follow him. Christians today do not have followers largely because they do not know where they themselves are going. Contrast this with Jesus in John 13:3-4. He could serve his disciples because he knew where he had come from and where he was going. One who knows his purpose in life will find that others will be willing to follow him.

Faithfulness is another quality in the personable relationship. We cannot expect to lead others beyond our own level of commitment. Unfaithfulness in the life of a disciple-maker is just as easily reproduced as is faithfulness. It is not entirely that we are not reproducing disciples in the church. Due to our unfaithfulness, we are reproducing the wrong kind of disciples. We have to be consistently faithful on every front of our lives as we seek to train followers. Remember, they are watching us and they copy what they see. We cannot help but reproduce what we are.

Longsuffering is also passed on through up-close relationships. This is the quality in the life of the disciple-maker that allows him to forbear with his disciples. We can quickly become discouraged with our disciples as the apostles were to Paul, and as Paul was to John Mark. When the ignorance or immaturity of the disciple shows up, it is easier to toss him aside than to go through the trouble of tearing down the negative things in order to build up the positive things. Longsuffering allows us to put up with the young disciple until his transformation takes place.

Love is the central quality of the personable relationship. How many close relationships have you ever seen without it? This is the highest form of love; the God-kind of love. This is the kind of love that gives of itself, does what is best, and brings out the best in the one who is the object of that love. This is the kind of love that allows us to lay down our lives for the brethren. It is known in too few places today.

The remainder of Paul's list is where it really gets tough to be a disciple-maker. The first half of the list seems to be the ideal conditions that build disciples. The second half can appear to be enemies that hinder us from performing these ideals. *Patience* is a quality that is to be found in a close relationship. There is a difference in longsuffering and patience. Longsuffering is what the disciple-maker has for the disciple. Patience is what the disciple-maker has for himself. To be patient is to be cheerful under a load. This is so important because the next three qualities speak of how heavy the load can become. To be cheerful under the load is not to ignore the

55

load or pretend it is not there. To be cheerful under the load is to live as if we believe that Jesus Christ is bigger than any load or problem that may present itself to us. Cheerfulness under the load means that I am trusting Christ to help me work through my situation. This dispels worry and fosters trust and confidence in the lives of our disciples. They need to see, as Paul said, "None of these things move me...that I might finish my course with joy."(Acts 20:24).

Paul did not hide his *persecutions* from Timothy in their relationship. We should never convey to those who follow us that there is no cost involved as we follow Christ. The New Testament teaches that we should expect to be persecuted as we belong to Christ Jesus. Persecution pursues us to try to keep us from fulfilling our ministry and place within the body of Christ. We should let our disciples see when we are persecuted and how we handle it. They need to learn this so they can make it through their persecutions also.

Within the personable relationship, we can show our disciples something of our *afflictions* as an ambassador of Christ. This actually speaks of two kinds of afflictions. First, those on the outside that may cause us physical harm or pain. Second, the emotional pain or afflictions that we feel on the inside as a result of the task that God has given us to accomplish. In 1 Corinthians 11, Paul spoke of each of these. He certainly had physical afflictions, shown by the very brand marks on his body from stonings, whippings and beatings. But he also felt an inner struggle when he saw the spiritual needs of others. As we take on the responsibility of building disciples for world impact, we should expect to have both kinds of afflictions. The way we handle them will determine if our followers stay with us or not

Timothy also learned of Paul's *endurance* as they shared their personable relationship. He had seen Paul, under heavy burdens, bear them from underneath. God himself had helped shoulder the load. Endurance is a quality that disciples have to learn, first, from someone who is doing it. It does not come naturally. Everything within our flesh wants to run when the going gets tough. John Mark showed us that our natural bent is to run from the struggle rather than to bear up underneath it. Endurance needs to be seen in our lives and reproduced in the lives of our disciples.

Finally, Paul was able to relate his *deliverances* to Timothy as they walked together in the ministry. Timothy learned that God was near to help and deliver, indeed, to preserve the disciple's life until his work on earth was complete. Ultimate deliverance then comes when that work is done and God takes us home to be with him. Paul spoke of that deliverance by saying, "For to me, to live is Christ, and to die is gain."

Try this exercise with this text. Take the eleven qualities of the personable relationship and align them, the first with the last and so on until you meet in the middle. Here's what you will see.

Doctrine - Deliverance

Manner of life - Endurance

Purpose - Afflictions

Faithfulness - Persecutions

Longsuffering - Patience

Love

What we believe brings about our ultimate deliverance. We can endure anything if we live the right kind of lifestyle. Our purpose can be accomplished regardless of whatever afflictions we may have. We have to be faithful in all of our persecutions. We can only be longsuffering with others if we know patience with ourselves. All of this together shows us how we can love others in personable relationships that help to equip them for their own personal ministry for God. By cultivating a personal relationship with Jesus Christ, and personable relationships with other people, disciples can be reproduced who will be able to fulfill Christ's commission in just the way that he intended it to be fulfilled.

A PERSONAL TESTIMONY IN DISCIPLE-MAKING

The method of conquering the world that we learn from the Scriptures is that we have a close relationship with Christ and also with someone we can learn from. The purpose of this method is to turn us into a leader that others can follow. Once we have been trained by our disciple-maker, we are to take on that responsibility with another new or struggling Christian. We have to be fed until we can feed ourselves and then feed others. This kind of personal togetherness has been all but eliminated in many of our local churches today. We do not want others to know or bother us and we do not want to know or bother them.

We have become isolated in our own little worlds of loneliness, inwardly crying out for a close relationship while maintaining a glossy front that says to others, "I have it all together." Let's see if I am right. Do you have even one friend in the ministry that you can be totally honest with? No matter what you tell that person, he will listen to you and not judge you or gossip your deepest secrets to others. Is there one person in your life who has assumed the responsibility to see that you make it in your walk with Christ? Do you have one person that you can depend on who will give you his time at any time, day or night, to help you with your personal development? Has even one Christian invited you to follow them and copy their lifestyle as a Christian? Do you know one who is making an impact on the world for Christ by following the commission to build reproducing disciples? Do you have one who has partnered with you in ministry to believe God for world impact? If you do, you are blessed and fortunate. For the majority of you who do not know such a person, you need to find one. They are there. You just have to locate one. Then, you have to become one for others who need someone to get in front and lead the way.

My story as a Christian is like many of yours. I was raised in a Southern Baptist Christian home along with two brothers and two sisters. Our parents loved the Lord and had us in church at any opportunity. At the age of six, I was saved on a Sunday morning at church. For the next eight or so years, I continued to be a regular attendee at church. I went to Sunday School, Training Union, and

Vacation Bible School. I sat through at least three sermons a week as well as numerous revival meetings. I had learned many of the stories of the Bible and could answer all of the questions asked by my teachers. I had even suspected that God was calling me into the pastoral ministry. However, it seemed that going to church, learning Bible stories, being good and "giving a small portion of what God has blessed us with" was all there was to this being saved. While a good foundation was given to me there, I never learned a reason for it all. I was all tanked up but had no idea where to go or what to do next.

When I was about fourteen years old, I began to find other things to get involved in. I saw no larger context for my life in Christ than to attend church. Looking back, not one Christian ever enlisted me to follow them as they followed Christ in a personal ministry to the world. They just said be in church and be good. Having no direction as a Christian, I fell out of church and turned to the world, hoping to find a place to fit in and belong. There was a deep longing and desire in my heart but I did not know what it was there for or how to listen to it. God allowed me to wander in a wilderness of sin for another ten years before he began to do some major reconstruction in my life. At this point, I had been saved for eighteen years but was no more prepared to serve God than I was the day before I was saved.

I started to attend church again with Connie while we were dating. We had a wonderful pastor, Bill Pate, who helped me begin to walk with God. He was always available to me when I wanted to ask questions. He also had printed notes on many of the subjects that we talked about. He was a great help to me in those days of beginning my search for my place in the body of Christ.

While we were there at Tucapau Baptist Church, we called Chris Balltzglier as our youth minister. Chris and I became instant friends. He invited me to go to a Bible Conference hosted by his family at Mt. Gilead Baptist Church in Griffin, Georgia. As I walked into the church that evening, Herb Hodges was speaking about the kind of man that Jesus chooses to be a world-impacting disciple-maker. There was something in what he was saying and in the way he was saying it that spoke to me to the core of my being. In my spirit, I was saying, "This is it! This is what I have needed to see and hear all of my Christian life." God had begun to turn the light on in my spirit to let me see from his point of view.

I listened to all of the preachers in that conference but most attentively to brother Herb. All of them had something to say but Herb had something to say to me. I wanted to meet him but reasoned that since he was an international speaker, I would be just another hand-shake. Boy, was I wrong! Chris introduced me to him and he received me not only with open arms but also with an open heart. I was floored! For the first time in my life, I had met a Christian who knew where he was going to take a personal interest in me.

We began to correspond through the mail and on the telephone. The personal letters that Herb wrote to me served as great training tools. I asked him for a crash course in disciple-making. He sent fourteen cassette tapes to me with messages about the process of building personal disciples, just like Jesus did. I listened to those tapes over and over, writing the messages word for word, memorizing the process. He also recommended some specific titles for reading. I read those books as well as everything else I could get my hands on about disciple-making. Under his guidance, I searched the Bible and began to see the standard of disciple-making on nearly every page. My vision was transformed from just having light to having illumination. Over the years, Herb and I have also spent many hours together cultivating our relationship. We have prayed together, went to church, played golf, went fishing, watched movies, shopped and shared meals. I had the great privilege to accompany him on a mission trip to the Philippines in 1996.

In 1992, brother Herb spoke in my pastorate in Orangeburg, South Carolina, staying with us in our home for a week. He had just returned from South Africa and he had the name of a man on a piece of paper who had asked him for study material on the Tabernacle of the Old Testament. I had a brand new workbook about the Tabernacle on my bookshelf. I mailed it to Gilbert Nkomo in South Africa, beginning an international ministry called Regal Resources.

Regal Resources has chosen our theme verse to be (1 Corinthians 16:15) which says "The household of Stephanas made up their minds to devote their lives to looking out for Christian brothers." Through the years, God has used this ministry to provide Bible study and disciple-making materials to pastors and potential leaders around the world. We have paid the full tuition for a pastor and his wife to go to the seminary for four years in Davao City, Philippines. We are currently supporting two national pastors in the Philippines, one who is working among the tribal Mansaka people, some of whom have already been saved and are being discipled. We helped to provide the resources to build a small building for the church there to worship in. Our Bible studies are also in about forty countries all over the world via the internet.

God is still wondrously developing this ministry into much more than I ever dreamed of. We are in the processes of developing our own written and recorded discipling resources. We are developing a radio program called "The Great Commission Broadcast" on which we will only discuss disciple-making topics. We are developing a conference called "The Great Commission Conference" by which we introduce churches to the process of building disciples. God is also opening doors for us to present the conference to families in their homes.

In addition to these blessings, God has allowed me the privilege to spend many hours with faithful men and women who are doing the same with others also. It is a wonderful thing to see the light come on in a person's spirit as they begin to see God's purpose for their lives, their potential and how His power can work in their lives.

Allen L. Elder

I have to say beyond the shadow of a doubt that the most significant occurrence in my Christian life has been and is my relationship with Herb Hodges. Not just because it's Herb, but because of what I have seen of Jesus in and through Herb. I have learned that I can fulfill the great commission every day of my life. I have learned that through reproducing my own personal representatives, my life can count to the last person on earth till the end of time. I have learned the purpose for which God saved me and for which I am to live each day of my life. Through him, I have learned to use the method Jesus used and taught in order to build disciples of Christ for world impact. It is available to anyone who wants their life to make a significant mark on the world for God's glory.

PART TWO

BUILDING CURRICULUM

Allen L. Elder

CHAPTER FOUR

THE DISCIPLE-MAKER

(Ecclesiastes 12:9-11)

In the previous section, I briefly overviewed the process of fulfilling our Lord's great commission by building personal, reproducing disciples. This has been, by no means, an exhaustive attempt on the subject. Many volumes exist, written by those much more capable than I, that ought to be in the believers ongoing reading list. This attempt has been meant merely to serve as an introduction to disciple-making for new-comers and a reminder for those already exposed to the process, while laying a foundation for this section of this present work.

Section two is really the aim of this book. It has been my experience, as well as my observation of others who were newly enlightened to the subject of disciple-making, to ask the obvious question once they had been exposed, "How do *I* do this? and Where do I start?" My aim in writing this book is to suggest a starting place and to encourage a life-long practice of building curriculum studies for the purpose of building disciples. I intend to offer my own personal system of gathering, filing and retrieving teaching material to use over and over again as we have the privilege to work with different disciples. This system works very well for me and I believe it can be of help to any pastor, teacher, or disciple-maker. It needs to be noted that while I have used these training objectives (as I like to call them) many times, I have never used them in the same order twice. Discipling has to fit the need of the individual at the time. All of the subjects eventually need to be presented but we have to begin with the disciple's most immediate need.

Disciple-making is an up-close, personal relationship in which one person invests his life into another person, reproducing and multiplying his life with the goal of impacting the world for Christ to the last person on earth until the end of time. Building disciples is all about building relationships. Building disciples through building relationships requires that we also build curriculum. We must have Biblical subjects ready to teach that can be tailored to meet the needs of any potential disciple. Ecclesiastes 12:9-11 takes a look at the two individuals involved in the personable relationship; the disciple-maker and the disciple. It also looks at their responsibilities toward each other. Let's look first of all at the disciple-maker.

THE WISE MAN

In the text, we are given two characteristics of an effective disciple-maker. To begin with, he is a wise man. We often equate wisdom with age. We say that if one is old, he must also be wise. This is not necessarily true. I know some older people who are more foolish now than when they were young. The truth is, a person can be young and wise at the same time. Wisdom is seeing things from God's point of view. As we read the Word of God and ask God for wisdom, he will give it to us if we plan to use it for God's glory. If we are going to be teachers, if we are going to make disciples, we have to see things from God's perspective. We have to be wise men and women.

Our passage also tells us three practices of a wise teacher or disciple-maker. First he has to be a communicator of truth: "He went on teaching the people." An elderly pastor friend told me the story of a friend of his and a young man in his congregation who said he had been called to preach. The young man's pastor told him that they would give him the opportunity to preach his first sermon in the church very soon. The day came for him to deliver the sermon. He stood up in the pulpit and said, "And whatsoever you sow, that shall you also reap." He stood there a few minutes and said again, "And whatsoever you sow, that shall you also reap." A few more minutes went by and he said a third time, "And whatsoever you sow, that shall you also reap." Then he turned to his pastor and said, "Come get her Pat, she ain't what I thought she was." Preaching and teaching requires much preparation. Communicating truth requires that diligent study be a constant discipline of the disciple-maker. We have to have a regular exposure to the Word of God by listening to sermons, reading, personal Bible study and prayer. As we expose ourselves to truth, God will see to it that we always have some fresh bread to present to others.

Another practice the disciple-maker must develop is the collecting of teaching material. We must always be on the look-out for ways to present the truth to our disciples. A friend told me early in my ministry, "If you ever stop reading, you'll be dead in the water." Reading the ideas and thoughts of others stimulates our own. My mentor, Herb Hodges, taught me a valuable tool to use as I read. When I read a book and find outlines, illustrations, etc..., I write them down with page reference on the inside front cover of the book. When I finish reading the book, all I have to do is open the front cover to scan it for teaching materials that I have gleaned. This practice is very helpful in sermon or lesson preparation. Once, while on vacation in Florida, I read *Multiplying Disciples* by Waylon Moore. I had filled the inside cover of the book by the end of the week. This book is one that every Christian needs to keep close at hand for regular review and reference.

Teaching material can be found in many places. Reading, of course, but also while listening to sermons on tape, radio or television. Movies, believe it or not, can be a great source of teaching insights. Herb and I once watched a Robin Williams movie from a disciple-making perspective and found a plethora of important traits of a leader of students. Sporting events and conversations with others can provide an abundance of illustrations and commentaries on Scripture verses that God brings to our minds. All of these need to be recorded and made ready for retrieval.

That, in fact, is the third practice of a wise teacher according to this focal passage. He not only communicated truth, and collected teaching material, but he classified them for ready reference. When I first began in the ministry, I had a terrible way of collecting notes that I had made. When I heard a sermon in church, for example, I took notes on a piece of paper. When I went home, I dropped the paper into a cardboard box. I had no way of knowing what was in the box or where to find a particular piece of information without dumping it out and looking at each piece of paper until I found what I was looking for. Needless to say, this was a huge time waster. Anything we collect needs to be organized so we can use it in a moments notice. It does us little good to collect material if we do not also classify or organize it.

Classification helps us to file and retrieve any teaching material we may have on any subject. It helps us identify areas in which we need more material. It gives us ready access to any text or topic we may need to teach. Training objectives are the subjects used to classify our material. They serve several purposes, too. Training objectives organize our works in a systematic way. They can be used to guide us in the building of disciples. They help us to evaluate the growth and progress of our disciples. They help our disciples to learn how to organize their own material to teach their disciples. Classification of training objectives is a must for every wise disciple-maker.

A GOOD TEACHER

The disciple-maker is not only a wise teacher who communicates, collects, and classifies teaching material. He is also a good teacher. We all have ideas about what makes someone a good teacher. Someone who is able to make masterful use of illustrations may be considered a good teacher. A person who knows Greek and Hebrew may be considered a good teacher by someone else. Yet another person may be said to be a good teacher who makes wonderful practical application of the Word of God. All of these certainly enhance a teachers ability to teach. However, the text simply says that a good teacher is a person who just teaches what he knows.

After coming out of the Air Force, I became the store manager of a retail lumber yard. While there, I developed a love for cabinet-making. I tried to build a few pieces of furniture to try out my new hobby. I began with what I knew to do. Some of those first pieces were not the best work I ever did but they served their purpose. As time went on, I practiced more, talked with other cabinetmakers, read more about the craft, and was able to build better cabinets. If I had not started with what I knew, I would not have been able to make any more progress.

Teaching is like that. A good teacher just teaches what he knows. That is the starting place. As we begin to teach someone, we soon learn that we do not know very much about Christ and the Bible. There is no problem with that as long as we do what Jesus told us to do, "Take my yoke upon you and learn of me." (Matthew 11:29). All we have to do is to get one step ahead of our disciple and move out. It is like walking in the dark with a flash light. We walk within the area where we have illumination. The more we walk, the more pathway ahead becomes illuminated before us. As we begin with what we know and continue to study, God gives us more light and understanding that we can pass on to our disciples.

As I write this portion of this book, I am sitting on a balcony, enjoying a cool breeze, overlooking Coquina Harbor and the Myrtle Beach Yacht Club. No, it isn't mine. It is borrowed for the week. It is a beautiful harbor with modern condominiums on every side, manicured landscapes, with a boardwalk around the entire harbor which is complete with a lighthouse. People are on the boardwalk getting their morning exercise, walking or jogging. In the harbor, at dock after dock, are all kinds of boats. Some are very large and expensive. Others are sailing-craft. Still more are smaller, even jet skies and motorized rubber rafts. Each ship is, no doubt, a sea-worthy vessel, equipped with engines, radar and lifeboats. Occasionally, one of the yachts will leave its dock and slowly move out to the intracoastal waterway, a pathway to the Atlantic Ocean. As I have watched this scene morning after morning, it reminds me of so many potential teachers and disciple-makers who already know something they could pass on to others. Yet they sit like beautiful ships in a harbor. Ships that someone paid a very high price for, but sit day after day collecting barnacles, tied to their docks, showing little or no sign of life around them. Only every now and then will someone leave the port to take the adventurous voyage of teaching and training other disciples to become reproducers. Like these ships in the harbor, I wonder how many people spend more time tied to the dock than they spend on the seas of life, helping others to learn to navigate the open waters. We should be more like Paul who said, "So naturally, we proclaim Christ! We warn everyone we meet, and we teach everyone we can, *all that we know about him,* so that, if possible, we may bring every man up to his full maturity in Christ Jesus." (Colossians 1:28)Phillips.

A good teacher teaches what he knows but he also teaches in an interesting manner. One teacher may thoroughly know a subject but bore us to tears with his teaching. Solomon said, " A wise teacher makes learning a joy." (Proverbs 15:2) Living Bible. This is the kind of teacher who not only knows the subject, but knows how to communicate it so his disciples can know it, too. In high school algebra, I was completely lost. My teacher might as well have been speaking a foreign language to me. I struggled through the class barely getting by. But in college, my algebra teacher knew how to get me to understand it. She sat down personally with me, time and again, and helped me to know some of what she knew. I have had the same experience in the church. Those teachers who have captured my interest have made learning a great joy for me. Jesus was the most interesting teacher who ever taught. His class was always in session whether in a synagogue, by the lake shore, or on a mountainside. He used any available object nearby to illustrate his teaching and capture the interest of his disciples. He often used illustrations from fishing, farming, or flowers to get his message across to them. This wise method of teaching allows us as the teacher to be free, not bound by a traditional classroom setting. We only have to know the subject and be ready to apply it to any environment we may happen to be in when the opportunity to teach presents itself.

We must also remember that teaching is a spiritual gift. Romans 12:11 tells us of two responsibilities a teacher must fulfill in his teaching ministry. The teacher must work hard at his teaching. He cannot be lazy, either in his preparation or in his presentation. Lazy teachers lose their audiences. Then, the teacher must be enthusiastic. I cannot imagine anything to become more enthusiastic about than building reproducing disciples for world impact. Nothing else holds a candle to this task. Enthusiastic teaching will help us to be mindful of the fact that as we teach, we are not just teaching lessons, we are teaching people. As we spend time with them, teaching them, they will catch our vision for the world. Enthusiasm creates an environment of contagion. Regardless of how well we may teach, if the commission has not captured our enthusiasm, why should it capture that of the listeners? If we will show some enthusiasm, our disciples will be more able to catch that desire and vision from us.

A good disciple-maker has to be wise as he communicates, collects, and classifies truth to present to his disciples. He also has to be a good teacher, teaching what he knows in an interesting manner, conditioned by hard work and enthusiasm. The disciple is no less responsible. The next chapter will address the disciple's responsibilities as a student in the up-close, personable relationship.

CHAPTER FIVE

THE DISCIPLE

As an occupation, I work as a draftsman and in sheet-metal layout for a mechanical, industrial contractor. I am also a bi-vocational pastor. My experience in pastoring and teaching in the church has now extended into sixteen years. In these years, I have spoken to an audience of listeners literally thousands of times. Each time I speak, I am always amazed at the number of people in the congregation who make very little effort to capture what is being presented to them. To me, it has always seemed so inefficient for a teacher or pastor to spend hours in preparation for a sermon, message, or lesson that is delivered in thirty to forty-five minutes and is then gone forever. Gone forever because the teacher often feels inferior if he repeats a sermon or uses the same outline more than one time. Gone forever, also, because the audience has made little or no effort to learn or record for the purpose of presenting to someone else that which has been given to them. Disciples have a great responsibility to fulfill each time truth is communicated to them. I think Waylon Moore said it best when he said, "The congregation is just as responsible to leave with the sermon as the pastor is to arrive with it." Our text tells us how a disciple can do that.

In the first place, a disciple has a responsibility to heed the teacher's words. As disciples, we need to hear what our discipler is saying to us. The old saying is true, "Telling isn't teaching and listening isn't learning." Just because we listen does not mean that we hear. Jesus had a lot to say about hearing. He said be careful *that* you hear; be careful *how* you hear; and be careful *what* you hear. Hearing is so important because the root word is also the word for obedience. We cannot properly obey if we do not properly hear.

Verse eleven gives us two reasons why we should heed and hear our teacher's words. We should heed and hear our teacher's words because they nail down important truths. I still find it amazing the number of times pastors and teachers have nailed down important truths, and because of poor listening, the audience cannot re-present that teaching five minutes after it has been delivered. As a result, we see people who are still unsure of their salvation, unable to briefly present most Biblical doctrines, still ineffective in their witness, no sense of direction, and still not reproducing disciples. We must heed our teachers because the truth they nail down brings assurance into our lives. As we hear truth, see it in the Word of God, and receive it, it provides the assurance we need and fosters confidence in our hearts when that area of our lives is under fire. Nailed down truths also produce liberty in our lives. As we know the truth, it sets us free (John 8:32). It takes the truth of God's Word to tear down strongholds, attitudes, and unbelief in our hearts. We should heed our teachers words because of the truths they nail down for us.

Another reason to heed our teacher's words is that they are like goads that spur us to action. A person driving a team of oxen kept an ox goad nearby. When the oxen stopped or strayed, the driver would poke him with the goad to make him go ahead in the right direction. Our teachers words motivate us many times to do things God has called us to do. We know we need to do the work but for whatever reason, it has not been done. So the teacher has to spur us to action. We are moved to action in several ways. First, because they make the truth personal to us. All of the doctrine in the Bible will do us no good if it does not become personal to us. The aim of God's Word is to change us, to conform us to the image of Christ. In order for this to happen, truth has to become personalized. It has to make us look at our own lives in the light of Scripture and from God's point of view. Anything we see in that light that is out of focus with the Word has to be conformed. The first action our teacher's words should motivate us to is to change anything in our lives that is out of line as it is revealed when truth becomes personal to us.

Our teacher's words move us to action also because they make the truth practical. I realize that God reserves the right to have us do things that may seem illogical to ourselves or to others. I am sure Naaman did not think it was very logical or practical to dip himself seven times in the murky Jordan River in order to be cleansed of leprosy. He did it because this is what God's man prescribed for him to do. It seems to me that the far-out instructions that God gives to some are often commensurate with our own far-outness to his plans. Many people today think God always wants us to be far-out and weird in the way we dress, serve and respond to him personally. God, however, would rather deal with us in practical terms. His desire is to do things decently and in order, the same that he requires of us. Nothing more effectively motivates people to do God's work according to his will than plain, practical instructions from the Word of God. We often wish that God's leading were like it was for David and others of old who inquired of the Lord by an ephod, or Urim or Thummim, or through a prophet or priest and God told them, step by step, exactly what to do. Today, all these things have been fulfilled in a person, Jesus. As we walk closely with him, heeding the practical words of our teachers, he teaches us how to see from his perspective, find his leading, and make the right decisions. It all begins when we heed and hear the personal, practical truths taught by our disciple-makers.

Our teachers also motivate us to action as their words help to develop character qualities in our lives. They help us to reach our potential. Their words take us from where we are to where we need to go. We are motivated to think, and dream and reach and stretch until we see the bigger picture of purpose and strive to make it reality on a personal level. I believe that the one thing that is lacking in Christian circles today are the up-close, personable relationships in which a disciple-makers words are so conveyed to disciples that they nail down important truths and spur disciples to action that moves them into the realm of world impact. So much is at stake, hinging on heeding and hearing the words of a disciple-maker.

As disciples, we are not only responsible to heed and hear our teacher's words, but we are also responsible to master what our teachers tell us. Jesus himself set the standard here. He said, "I do nothing of myself, *but as my Father hath taught me*, I speak these things." (John 8:28). The only way to master our teacher's words is to do all we can to get those words. I like to think of mastering a teacher's words with three "R's". Mastering teaching that is given to us begins with *recording* it. One of the most discouraging scenes to me personally as a teacher is to present teaching to people who have no intention of recording it. They depend on their listening alone to record the message. This is futile because we cannot hear everything that is being said in one sitting. A friend of mine had a lady to take the tapes of his sermons and transcribe them each week. She said that she was surprised, as she listened to the tapes, to realize that she did not hear many of his statements when the message was originally delivered. Sometimes it takes several listenings to hear what is being said. On the other hand, a most encouraging scene are those people with paper and pencil in hand, following along, recording all they can get hold of. The difference between these two types of listeners is that one has no intention to do anything with the truth. He is content to let it blow past him without taking any responsibility for it. The other listener intends to use it in a couple of ways. First, in his own life. After recording his notes, he then has the capacity of doing further research in private devotions. One lady told me that the notes she takes from my sermons provide starting places for her daily devotions. Another lady takes notes during the message in her own handwriting, then goes home and types them on her computer. Second, the disciple can arrange the material to suit his own style in order to present it to someone else. Truth presented always has two aims: to stop in us long enough to affect a change then to be passed on by us to another person. Recording the truth as it is presented is the only way to do that.

Another "R" that helps us master our teacher's words is to *rehearse* the truth after it has been recorded. Rehearsing requires three simple exercises. To begin with, we must study what we have received. This helps us come to our own understanding and conviction about the truth. We have to be like the Christians at Berea who searched the Scriptures daily to see if Paul had told them the truth. We need to take the text that is exegeted, read it, look at our notes, see the practical application and let it settle into our hearts to do it's work in our lives. Once we have studied the material, understanding it with the amount of light we have at that time is the next step. We need to have confidence in what we say we believe. Understanding promotes confidence and confidence promotes sharing with others what we know.

The final step in rehearsing truth is to arrange it the way we would like to present it to someone else. We all have our own style of organization and delivery. A young man once said to his pastor after hearing his sermon, "I know where you got that sermon. It is from such-and such book." The pastor, not being intimidated at all said, "My philosophy is that if it fits my gun, I'm going to shoot it." We need a like philosophy in our teaching.

The last "R" is to *repeat* to others what we have received. We are not only to receive truth but also to reproduce it. We have to pass it on. Jesus expected his disciples to teach what they were taught in pure form, just the way they had received it. This preserves the truth for future generations. Jesus said, "When the disciple is fully trained, he will be like his teacher." (Luke 6:40). Paul said to Timothy, "And the things that thou hast heard of me among many witnesses, the same commit thou to faithful men, who shall be able to teach others also." (2Tim 2:2). Mastering what the disciple-maker teaches us is important because it follows the example set by Jesus and used by other disciple-makers in the Bible. Following this pattern ensures the fulfillment of the great commission.

A disciple is responsible to heed and hear his teacher's words and master them. By doing this, he becomes a personal representative of his teacher. As he goes throughout the world building disciples, he not only represents Jesus, but also, his disciple-maker. When Paul sent Timothy to the Philippians, he said, "It will be as if I myself were there with you." He could say that with all confidence because Timothy, the young disciple, had mastered everything Paul had given him. Wise and good teachers along with students who hear, master, and reproduce what they have been taught create the environment in which people are trained to obey the lord's mandate to build disciples on a world-wide scale.

CHAPTER SIX

THE DISCIPLE-MAKERS NOTEBOOK

If we are going to be good teachers who are going to wisely communicate truth to our disciples, we have to collect and classify that truth in some way that allows us to know where it is and retrieve it for use when we need it. Over the years, I have tried to develop the habit of keeping three specific notebooks; one for sermons; one for devotional thoughts or sermon starters; and one for disciple-making. All of the notebooks are basically set up in the same manner but are used in different ways. This practice has worked very well for me therefore I would like to suggest it to everyone who desires to be an organized, effective teacher and maker of disciples.

THE SERMON NOTEBOOK

First, let's look at the sermon notebook. I am a firm believer that if a sermon is worth preaching one time, it is worth preaching many times. We can use our sermons in many different ways. Any sermon can also be incorporated into a group of sermons which could be used as a series of messages on a particular subject. We can keep them on file to give to people who ask about a particular passage of Scripture. The same sermon can be used to share with different groups within the church and even rearranged to share with those who have already heard it. We should not be so foolish as to think that just because we said it, the people heard all of it. Do not be intimidated by repeating sermons for the purpose of teaching and training disciples. Jesus was not worried about repeating himself. In fact, he often did. He repeated himself, not because he did not have any new material, but so he could be sure that his disciples had learned what he wanted them to be able to give to the next people. Repetition is a valuable tool in making disciples.

Most preachers have their own method of making notes from which to preach. Some may use a hand-written or typed outline or full manuscript. Some preachers do not use notes at all in the pulpit. Personally, I use hand-written notes most of the time. I write then on loose-leaf notebook paper which allows me to do several things. Many times, my notes are written while I am on the go. I do not always have access to my computer so I write my thoughts down when I have sorted them out, wherever I may be. It helps me to present my thoughts in a logical, systematic manner that is easy for the listeners to understand and record. A written outline also keeps me on track while presenting the sermon. I do not like to chase the proverbial rabbits all over the Bible and the pulpit. Keeping my notes this way also provides a record of what I have preached. I can review it from time to time to see what subjects I have overcooked or which areas that I need to give more attention to. It allows me to file the sermon for future reference. We should never throw away our notes. That is like arriving at a far away destination after a long journey only to discover that you used your map as fire starter along the way. There may be times when I want to review a passage again for myself, or I may want to give the notes to someone who wants to study that subject. While preaching, I generally use an expanded outline, but not a full manuscript. Later, I sometimes write the manuscript for those who want a copy of the sermon for themselves or to give away. Also, after I have about ten sermons, I can put them together in a collected works and make them available to serious students of the Word. All of these and other benefits are possible simply by carefully collecting and classifying your material.

Setting up a sermon notebook is very simple. All you need is binder of some sort, (I prefer the loose-leaf type) and a table of contents page at the front of each volume of sermons. You may want to limit the number of sermons that you store in each volume. The table of contents page shows with a glance, the sermons that are filed in each binder. All you have to do is record the sermon title and text refrence on the table of contents page, number the sermon note page with the appropriate number and file it in the binder. The sermons do not have to be in any particular order, by title or text. I usually file them in consecutive order as I deliver them. Once you deliver the sermon the first time, just log it, and file it, and it is stored for repeated use. Let's look at an example of a table of contents page from the sermon notebook.

TABLE OF CONTENTS

1. The Possibility of World Impact

(Eph. 1:15-19)

2. The Great Commission in Matthew

(Matt. 28: 18-20)

3. The Great Commission in Acts

Allen L. Elder

(Acts 1:8)

4. Multiplying Disciples

(2 Tim. 2:2)

By using this method of filing sermons, I can store as many sermons in a volume as I want to. Using the example above, let's say that my next sermon entry is *Building Personable Relationships* (2Tim 3:10-11). All I have to do to file this sermon is to turn to the table of contents page and log it in below the forth entry, write a number five in the upper, right-hand corner of the outline page, and place it in the binder behind sermon number four. The entry then looks like this.

TABLE OF CONTENTS

1. The Possibility of World Impact

(Eph. 1:15-19)

2. The Great Commission in Matthew

(Matt. 28: 18-20)

3. The Great Commission in Acts

(Acts 1:8)

4. Multiplying Disciples

(2 Tim. 2:2)

5. Building Personable Relationships

(2 Tim 3:10-1

I like this method of filing sermons because it is expandable. All I have to do is to keep adding to it. It also allows me to carry with me a number of sermons that are already prepared and ready to use as the Holy Spirit guides and opens doors for preaching.

THE DEVOTIONAL NOTEBOOK

The second notebook that I use and enjoy is what I refer to as a devotional notebook. In this book, I record devotional thoughts, ideas that I have, or insight that the Holy Ghost gives me as I read the Word of God. I can use these thoughts for sermon starters as I seek God's will in what I should preach. This notebook is large and is set up a little differently than the sermon notebook. My devotional book is a three inch binder. It has a divider for each book of the Bible. As your entries grow in number, you may have to consider a binder for each book of the Bible, or perhaps one for the Old Testament and one for the New Testament. The dividers are labeled in order from Genesis to the Revelation. After each divider is a table of contents page, much like the one in the sermon notebook. It also allows for ongoing expansion. As I read the Bible and God speaks to me about something from a particular verse, I record it and file it in my devotional notebook. On the table of contents page, I make the entry number, assign a subject, and record the text from the Bible. As I do this, I am essentially writing my own commentary on the Bible. With this notebook available to me, when I consider preaching from any text, I can look it up in the appropriate table of contents and see if I already have my own notes on that text. Or, if I want to teach on any subject, I can scan the table of contents for passages of Scripture and notes on that subject. I have found this to be a wonderful help to me in preparation for teaching. Another great aspect of the devotional notebook is that it represents time that I have personally spent alone with God. The entries in this book are what God has said to me. In a sense, it is a spiritual diary of my relationship with Christ. Let's look at an example of the table of contents and an entry in the devotional notebook.

MATTHEW TABLE OF CONTENTS

1. The Genealogies of Christ

(1:1-17)

2. The Incarnation of Christ

   (1:18-25)

3. The Identity of the Incarnate Christ

   (1:18)

4. The Intention of the Incarnate Christ

   (1:21)

5. Temptation

   (4:1-11)

6. Three Hindrances to Prayer

   (6:5-7)

7. The Model Prayer

   (6:9-13)

In the above example, let's say the next entry is The Prayer Closet (Matt 6:6). To file my notes, I would turn to the Matthew table of contents, mark entry number eight, write a number eight on the note page, and log it in the same way as the sermon notebook. Then I put the note page in the binder just after entry number seven. Get used to using your devotional notebook. It is one of the best secrets I have discovered in my relationship with Christ and in preaching and teaching his Word.

THE DISCIPLE-MAKER'S NOTEBOOK

The final notebook that I find to be of great help in the disciple-maker's notebook. This notebook is used for the strategic building of disciples. Of all the tools that I rely upon in building disciples, this notebook is the most important. Inside this book are the important things that a disciple needs to know in order to become a disciple-maker. I have developed my notebook over a period of years and still add to it on a regular basis. Here is how it is set up.

The disciple-maker's notebook has only five dividers. They are labeled as follows:

1. Training Objectives.

2. Disciple.

3. Discipline.

4. Discipler.

5. Discipling.

With the exception of Training Objectives, these sections are labeled after the vocabulary of disciple-making in the New Testament. A *disciple* is a follower of Christ who is learning to fulfill the great commission. *Disciplines* are the areas of life which reveal the cost involved in following Christ. A *discipler* is one who is building reproducing disciples and *discipling* is the process a discipler uses to make disciples. These definitions define the different classifications of collected teaching material (training objectives) that a disciple-maker must communicate to his disciples. They reveal what kind of training objectives should be filed in each division.

The training objectives division is simply a list of all of the objectives as they are classified in each of the four remaining dividers. Each training objective is listed under it's appropriate division. This serves as a quick reference in which division to find a specific topic for teaching. As new topics are entered, they are simply added to the appropriate list in the training objectives classification. Simply put, this section just gives the disciple-maker a quick look at what he has in his notebook. A training objectives page might look something like this.

Allen L. Elder

DISCIPLE	DISCIPLINE	DISCIPLING	DISCIPLER
1. Assurance of Salvation	1. Quiet time	1. Follow up	1. Strategy
2. Dealing with sin	2. Bible study	2. Great commission	2. Selection
3. Fellowship	3. Scripture memory	3. Multiplication	3. Association
4. The church	4. Meditation of Word	4. Disciple-making	4. Consecration
5. Spiritual Warfare	5. Prayer	5. Admonition	5. Impartation
6. The Bible	6. Evangelism	6. Teaching	6. Demonstration
7. Stewardship	7. Relational thinking	7. Your disciple	7. Delegation
8. Obedience	8. Temperance	8. Missionary team	8. Supervision

Each of the four remaining sections are set up in a similar way. Each section has it's own table of contents page and outlined training objectives ready for use in building disciples. Entries are made similarly to those in the sermon notebook and devotional notebook. Take a look at the example for some minor differences.

DISCIPLE TABLE OF CONTENTS

1. TO: Obedience

   SUB: 7 Benefits of obedience.

2. TO: Dealing with sin

SUB: Sin in the life of the Christian.

3. TO: The Bible

SUB: The Bible bookshelf.

This table of contents, like the others, is expandable. Limitless entries can be made in each division. This page tells me the number of outlined lesson plans that I have ready to teach from. It tells me the training objective (TO) that each entry addresses and the subject (SUB) of each ready-to-use outline.

Each entry in each division includes other important information. The top right-hand corner of the entry shows the entry number that corresponds with the table of contents. The first four lines of each entry tells me respectively, the division the entry belongs to, the training objective referred to, the subject of the lesson plan, and the source in which the information was found. After this information comes the outline to be used for teaching. At the end of the outline may be found references to other lesson plans on the same subject within the notebook. A scaled down example may look like this.

DISCIPLING 4-24

1. TO: Follow-up

2. SUB: 4 Methods of follow-up used by Paul.

3. REF: <u>Building Disciples Notebook</u>, by Waylon Moore. p.3.

4 Methods of Follow-up Used By Paul

   1. Personal Contact.

   2. Personal Intercession.

   3. Personal Representatives.

   4. Personal Correspondence.

I have used this system of collecting, and classifying teaching material for communicating the truth for the purpose of building disciples for more than ten years. It has proven to be one of the greatest discoveries that I have made as well as a most effective tool for building disciples. It is simple and easy to build upon. It houses all that a disciple needs to know in order to both be a disciple and make disciples. It can be taken along with the disciple-maker anywhere he goes. Keeping a disciple-making notebook is a discipline that any serious teacher would never regret. It makes building curriculum easier and more manageable as we build disciples.

CHAPTER SEVEN

WHAT TO DO WITH A DISCIPLE

Building reproducing disciples for world impact is the plan and passion of the Lord Jesus Christ for every one of his followers. The goal of this book has been to present that purpose to you as well as put within your hands a proven system of collecting and classifying teaching material for that strategic intent. Now that you have been shown what to do and given a way to do it, I want to suggest a place to begin.

In the first place, a difference should be noted between the *process* of making disciples and the *practice* of making disciples. There are many good books that focus on the process of disciple-making and it does require a specific process. Leroy Eims even called it "a lost art". I am compelled to say that we may present the process of building disciples over and over again and yet still not make a disciple.

When most people hear the process in presentation, they usually have one of two responses. One, they deny it's validity since it is so radically different from the traditional approach of the church. On the other hand, they may be so inspired and eager to climb aboard, they settle for learning to present the process to others and get them to do it as well. In this vein, the process is being presented but no disciples are being made. It is only when we use the process in an up-close, personal relationship that disciples are transformed and taught to reproduce. We must practice the process in order to build disciples.

The prophet Jeremiah offered a simple three-fold approach to practicing this process. In Jeremiah 1:10, he gave the following guideline: discover your disciple, develop your disciple which means tearing down as well as building up, and finally, deploy your disciple who will be trained to reproduce the same process in someone else.

There are basically two ways to discover a disciple; evangelize one or enlist one who has already been evangelized. Once you have begun your new relationship by either of the afore mentioned means, start working the process. Remember John chapter seventeen. Invite your disciple to join you in your own ministry for the Lord. Use the training objectives in your notebook to specifically tailor a plan for developing him into a reproducer. Impart your own vision for the world to him. Give him assignments that he can accomplish to check his accountability. Expect him to reproduce other reproducing disciple-makers. Your goal is reproduction. You are not finished until he can do this with another person. As you spend time with him, guide his growth and development, and give him an example to follow, you will soon see your life multiplied before your very eyes. With the making of just one disciple, you will have increased the value of your life by one hundred percent. Now, your disciple is ready to be planted, or deployed anywhere God chooses to plant him to build others.

A good place to begin in the development of your disciple is with a six-week training schedule. Invite him to meet with you for an hour or two for six consecutive weeks at a specified time and location. I have done this many times but never exactly in the same way. What you do in that six weeks is really determined by where your disciple is spiritually and what he needs at the time. Meet the immediate need first, then ask him to continue in disciple-making studies. Following are some suggested plans to use in a six-week study.

Allen L. Elder

Plan A - The ABC's of Christianity (Hebrews 6:1-2)

A - Salvation

Week 1 - All are sinners and in need of repentance.

Week 2 - Salvation by grace through faith.

B - Service

Week 3 - The works of the Holy Spirit.

Week 4 - Building personal disciples.

C - The State of Eternity

Week 5 - Final events.

Week 6 - Final estate of man.

Plan B - The Practical Process of the Christian Life (Thessalonians 1:5-10)

Week 1 - Saved through the gospel (v5).

Week 2 - Shaped by the gospel (v6).

Week 3 - Showcases of the gospel (v7).

Week 4 - Sharers of the gospel (8a).

Week 5 - Sent by the gospel (8b-10).

Week 6 - The 3-fold process of world impact (v6-8)

    1. Enlisted (v6).

2. Examples (v7).

3. Extension (v8).

Plan C - Selected Scriptures

Week 1- Sin.

Week 2 - Salvation.

Week 3 - Service.

Week 4 - Stewardship.

Week 5 - Spiritual gifts.

Week 6 - Strategy for world impact.

Plan D - The Master Plan of Evangelism by Robert Coleman - (8 weeks).

Study one chapter per week.

This six to eight week schedule will benefit you in several ways. You will be able to see if your disciple is going to make himself available to you at the specified times. As you give him reading and study assignments from week to week, you will be able to test his accountability to complete his work. You will know by the end of six weeks if he is determined and committed to a relationship of disciple-making. If he is not consistent for six weeks, it is a good indication that a long term commitment would not work. If he is consistent, you would want to suggest at the end of the cycle that you continue to meet for another cycle. Then you will eventually be able to move on to deeper teaching and discipleship training.

There is a specific plan to follow for building disciples. While we should cover all the basics with every disciple, we may do it dozens of different ways. I believe the only really wrong way is to not use the process at all. Building disciples is hard work and it takes time. But, it is the most important thing any Christian can do. To build disciples also requires that we build curriculum by which we train our disciples. If we will consistently collect and classify teaching material, we will be able to communicate God's truth in an efficient manner and trained, reproducing, world impacting disciples will be the results of our labor. Those who are doing this are the people which have accepted Jesus' offer of world conquest, and whose lives will be reproduced to the ends of the earth, until the end of time.

About the Author

Rev. Allen L. Elder has served Southern Baptist Churches in South Carolina for sixteen years. He has served in various ministries including Sunday School teacher, deacon, youth minister, education director, associate pastor, and pastor. Pastor Al is also the founder and president of Regal Resources, Inc., a non-profit organization devoted to providing disciple-making resources to disciple-makers all over the world. For some fifteen years, he has developed his ministry around the process of building personal disciples. He currently serves as a bi-vocational pastor of New Life Baptist Church, Woodruff, South Carolina and works in drafting and sheet-metal layout for Renfrow Brothers Mechanical Contractors. He, and his wife, Connie, have three sons, Trey, Blake, and Scott.

Printed in the United States
989900004B/217-297